Circling the Core

By the same author

POETRY COLLECTIONS

Fistful of Yellow Hope (Littlewood Press, 1984)
Cat Therapy (Littlewood Press, 1986)
Cathedral of Birds (Littlewood/Giant Steps, 1988)
Opening the Ice, with Ann Dancy (Smith/Doorstop, 1990)
Crossing Point (Littlewood Press, 1991)
Exits (Enitharmon Press, 1994)
The Panic Bird (Enitharmon Press, 1998)
Insisting on Yellow: New and Selected Poems (Enitharmon Press, 2000)
Multiplying the Moon (Enitharmon Press, 2004)
Becoming (SLP, 2007)

FICTION FOR CHILDREN AND TEENAGERS

Marigold's Monster (Heinemann, 1976)
If Only I Could Walk (Heinemann, 1977)
Will The Real Pete Roberts Stand Up (Heinemann, 1978)

BOOKS ABOUT WRITING

Writing for Self-Discovery, with John Killick (Element Books, 1998)
Writing My Way Through Cancer (Jessica Kingsley, 2003)

AS CO-EDITOR

Parents (Enitharmon Press, 2000)
Making Worlds (Headland, 2003)
Four Caves of the Heart (SLP, 2004)
Images of Women (Arrowhead Press, 2006)

Myra Schneider

Circling the Core

For Janet
with love
Myra
September 18
2008

ENITHARMON PRESS

First published in 2008
by Enitharmon Press
26B Caversham Road
London NW5 2DU

www.enitharmon.co.uk

Distributed in the UK by
Central Books
99 Wallis Road
London E9 5LN

Distributed in the USA and Canada
by Dufour Editions Inc.
PO Box 7, Chester Springs
PA 19425, USA

ISBN: 978-1-904634-66-9

Enitharmon Press gratefully acknowledges the financial support of
Arts Council England, London.

British Library Cataloguing-in-Publication Data.
A catalogue record for this book is available
from the British Library.

Designed by Libanus Press
and printed in England by
CPI Antony Rowe

ACKNOWLEDGEMENTS

Poems in this collection have appeared in:

Acumen, Agenda, Ambit, ARTEMISpoetry, Atlas, Dream Catcher, European Judaism, Faith And Freedom, The Forward book of poetry, 2008, The Frogmore Papers, Interpreter's House, Lapidus Quarterly, The London Magazine, Magma, The North, Nthposition online magazine, Babylon Burning: 9/11 Five Years On (Nthposition Press, 2006), *Orbis, Poetry London, Poetry Review, Quadrant* (Australia), *Quattrocento, The Reader, Scintilla, Second Light Newsletter, Trespass, Writing My Way Through Cancer* (Jessica Kingsley 2003).

'Core' won first prize in the Scintilla Poetry Competition 2004.

'Drought' won first prize in the Scintilla Poetry Competition 2007.

'Goulash' was shortlisted for the Forward Prize for Best Single Poem, 2007.

I particularly want to thank Mae Holsgrove for the cover painting, *The Rose*. Thanks also to the Elm Centre, a day opportunities drop-in centre in Dumbarton, Scotland run by Alzheimers Scotland, of which Mae was a member when she did the painting.

I would also like to thank the following people:
Erwin Schneider who unfailingly accepts that I am a compulsive writer and gives me an enormous amount of practical and emotional support; John Killick who for twenty-four years has given me feedback I trust on everything I have written; Mimi Khalvati for her rigorous, insightful and generous criticism; Mary MacRae for her thoughtful comments on poems at different stages; Caroline Price for comments on final versions of poems; the N7 workshop for helpful feedback; Stephen Stuart-Smith, my poetry publisher since 1994, for believing in my work and for all his support and consideration; Les Murray for his interest in my work and for publishing many of my poems in *Quadrant* during the last fifteen years.

'I cannot bite the day to the core.'

Edward Thomas, 'The Glory'

CONTENTS

CORE

ONE

after 'Hollow Form with Inner Form' by Barbara Hepworth

The shell is tall as a shed, shapely
as a human back travelling
down from shoulders through a poignant
hint of valley to two buttock mounds –
but this is a cylindrical world
winding inwards. If we cast off
edges and awkward corners, pick
the right word, will we be admitted
to the narrow passage whose sides
are ridged like an oak's, to the density
that darkens a keep? Surprisingly
nothing's locked, no notice forbids
trespassers. And look, an opening
that's easy beckons us to follow
the walls leaning protectively
as hooded women who are nursing
sobbing children. This rod standing
stone-still at the centre could be
jewel, kernel, womb, unshielded self,
a promise of continuance.
We lay hands on profound silence.

TWO

Forget the apples beginning to rot
on next door's tree, even the one dangling
so shiny and red over the fence. Forget
it shares the shape of newly discovered stars
billions of light years away, worlds whose matter
is hotter than we imagined possible.

Choose instead the small apple marooned on
a majolica dish bought in Amalfi
for its swirls of blue leaf and compact suns.
The russet skin is grainy as young bark
and smells of leaves – yellowed fingers that float
or flutter to sodden grass, sift into mush.

Feed on bracing white flesh, then ease a pip
bright as an eye from its slot, island it
on your palm, contemplate what it houses:
anchoring roots, tentative stem, silent
explosions of leaf, petals that whisper
pink, shrivel, leave nubs hard and green with future.

THREE

Not the pearl that murmurs
untroubled dreams of silk
and milkiness – that cool jewel
male poets once seized on
as a metaphor for teeth
or the loved one herself.

Not pearl, a smooth casing
the bi-sexual creature
makes to ease itself away
from sand grains and parasites
intruding between the lids
which hold it in a cool house.

Not the cased heart throbbing
as it pumps heat from room
to room, not the flames growing
behind the oven's glass door,
not even the intense
blue lick from filaments.

But the flesh within walls
that breathes, stirs, eats and makes –
the soft flesh so easily
stung, pecked or ripped apart.

FOUR

Tired of playing with sand, they thrust
puny spades into the grassless patch
beside their painted box, bypass

wriggles of chill flesh, lever stones
and hack at root claws. They're driven by
visions of the locked chest they'll prise

from the ground, its lid springing open,
gold pieces spilling into cupped hands,
rubies gleaming more darkly than blood,

a world which promises more than the stodge
of every day. Triumph is digging
a hole that's big enough to sit in.

They don't know it's less than a pinprick
in the earth's crust, that miles down under
rock-layers molten iron swirls

and within it spins a single
iron crystal almost the size
of the moon, not cold though – hot, hotter

than the burning sun. But as they dig,
eager for treasure, surely they sense
inner power, its immensity?

FIVE

Shearing hair, peeling skin, probing brain chambers
won't reveal my self. And it can't be caught
in the brightshine of a mirror angled
on my heart, trapped by fingers taking the pulse.

Is it a consciousness of warmth – the tie
with the few I'm close to, my love of that softly
gold fruit, generosity, a need for
uncooped sea, colour, or being alone?

Is it fear, pain in the body, a sense
of pain in the world we never stop wounding:
tree canopies, bitterns, lemurs, people –
or words and the silent webs they're hung in?

Today I see it as the chiff-chaff's nest
John Clare found, *built like an oven,* inside
soft as seats of down, a place where threads from
other lives are part of a new creation.

BIRD

after 'Stringed Figure (Curlew)' by Barbara Hepworth

I am wings
springing from breast, sweeping back, each curve echoing
the other. Meaning is space.
As I thrust forward my wingspan unnerves you. As I soar
do you yearn to encompass my power?

See how
I enfold head and heart in flight. Map out
my hungers and dangers, the complex of my parts. Feel my weight

and weightlessness,
bone mesh, skeins of blood, speckle and lie of feathers.
You will never explain the egg
where I began, dig out the deeply bedded knowledge
that guides me through dark and light.

Hold me down
and I will rise up above the crests on fierce waters,
above the sheer of rocks, above the heave and scramble of moors.

And I will be
here, there, within you, everywhere,
my flung wingtips longing to come together,
striving to complete a shape as I pierce and pierce the blue rush.

THE SILENCE IN THE GARDEN

for Dilys

No rule forbids speech but no one's talking. Quiet
grows from dark densities between boughs,
from heart-shaped leaves covering the ground,
their tight creamwhite umbrellas, flows

from spheres, spirals, hollows, undulations.
We come upon a hooded figure, trace spaces
that so poignantly speak her body. With hands
in a scoop that's river, wordlessly we unlace

the emerald hair of splayed weeds, silts
where fleshy roots bed, black threads
squirming from eggs. We don't need to name
the moment when twined swirls of bronze read

as petals unfolding outwards – corollas
frail as small birds' wings and as strong –
or the moment when a surge beneath the lid
makes the box of possibility spring

open. As if placing shoes outside a temple
we left our voices in the street by the gate,
entered another language. And now, sitting
by the untroubled waters, we dip feet.

Barbara Hepworth's garden, St Ives

BEACH

Insignificant as they are in this immensity
of shore, sea and sky the two horses
hypnotize me: craned heads leading
minute bodies, pin-thin legs
kicking up spray at the water's edge.

If I were close to I'd gaze at the moons
of chestnut buttocks, proud tails, conjure up
underbellies, myself lying in the path
of eight thudding hooves, their sweat
mingling mine. Would they swerve or trample?

But it's dusk, they are far away across
shingle, sands and long watertails
the tide cast off as it was tugged
back from land. I can wipe out
animals and riders with one thumb.

If that tiny person plodding along
the shoreline away from the horses
was within earshot I'd call out, ask
if she has rich pickings in her bags,
ask where I am and how to reach

the place I'm trying to find. Soon
she is fainter than the mist pinkening
the long sleeve of coast across
the bay. I sit down and for moments
so filled with clarity they become

an ever, I watch the horses, the ease
with which they cut through the slowly
deepening blue. The rising darkness
meets light seamlessly and it dawns
the name of this beach is acceptance.

LETTER FROM BIRSAY

Because you've never stood on this beach,
never breathed in this sea, I'll describe the sheet
after sheet of rock compressed into tilted layers,
the stones, bleached orange and ice blue,
lying in heaps and straggles, the ribboning sand,
the causeway leading to the island's green mound.

Because you will not visit this shore, because
you wouldn't see what I do if you did, I want you
to know how the smell of lime weed and salt
jumps me to a beach where water seeped into
our soft castles as we scrambled over rocks, knelt
to capture sleeping crabs and squirming eels.

Although this place, trekked by pilgrims who come
to climb to the island's church and look at outlines
of Viking houses, is miles to the north of the one
we shared, although we've lived decades in terrains
so apart no path could link them, on this beach
I half believe the one from long ago is in reach.

Although you misread, misunderstand me – neither
of us is in tune with the other's language – I am writing
to tell you how the sea scoops shells as it sweeps
over sand, wipes out the causeway, drowns rocks
and how, in spite of the dividing water, the island
is stitched to this shore fast as finger to hand.

HERON

Singleminded, it never lets go or perhaps
I don't – my eyes always skinned
for the flexing neck, the head streaked
with imperious black waiting to stab,
for the greyfold of wings over a frontage
white and terrible as soundlessness.

Sometimes it surprises me in the cold
of night, jointed legs pitched in lamplight
that the park's stream has neatly hooked,
its presence heightened as if I'd stumbled
into a dream flooded with significance
and was trying to cup torrents of feeling.

Sometimes I glimpse a snatch of white
behind willow leafiness and an eel
leaps inside me but it turns out to be
a plastic bag crucified on a branch
leaning over dirty water. Living
in its thrall saves me from the trap

of everyday. It inhabits that territory
where yellow heads become clocks
with ghostly parachutes, where wetness
rising after rain on hot afternoons
turns into genies of steam and dots
wriggling from spawn begin to breathe.

It inhabits channels that have swum free
from scum to catch the moon's thin edge
and depths with realities which no one
has fathomed – territories I can't resist
tapping, as if at an egg-shell, where the tock
of time, fear, possibility, all co-exist.

LET LOOSE

No edge to this living room.
A cerulean table is making love
to a floor that can't separate itself
from the walls and I am so immersed
in blue I could believe I've risen to the sky.

Who is the woman lounging on the mat
utterly at ease with haunches and the sprawl
of breasts? Would it be possible to lose
my gnawing self in such a worryless body?
Maybe I have. Maybe it's me toying

with the idea of fingering the vase,
its long narrow neck, me touching
the three tight flowers with petals
that are redder than painted lips.
Soaking in the bright heat, this naked

might-be me, is she passive, exultant,
empty-headed, excavating layers
of thought? Does she possess a soul?
The only reply is the door's sunflower-
yellow light. Donning a negligée,

I wander out onto the terrace, sniff
green tea leaves as they brew,
touch globes made of snowy flowerets,
gaze at gold tickling the lake's skin,
peaks clad in polar bear white.

I would believe freedom is composed
of these things if I could steer clear
of the newspapers shouting from the stall,
if I could forget the three fish indoors,
the crimson slices of their angry bodies

as they circle and circle their bulbous jar.
Over there is a slowly rising balloon.
I imagine myself in its basket, let loose
to float past mountains into the blue.
How long can I pretend it's unfettered?

VISION

All of a sudden I'm staring at my face,
a small clock that's out of joint
shouting from a wide waste of wall.
Its deeply divided state is ominous.

One side's recessed in bleak
turquoise shade, the other's flattened
by a blade of moon-whitened light.
To escape the coming confrontation I trek

from nose to mouthstrip, can't forget
the jet-black sun that wavers
in the shadow eye, how it radiates
sadness. If only I could untie its doubts.

The bright pupil sings the hill
of apple-green neck and I discover
my lost breast is restored, fuller
than before. It's then that I'm pulled

into the overgrown garden. What compels
are the huge unbroken faces feasting
on the sun's light, bees humming
at the crammed centres and growing silly

with nectar. These giants don't cry
greed, chew on yesterday's failures,
try to plan tomorrows. Unquestioning,
they live in the yellow blaze that's now.

IN THE FOREST

At last roadsound dies away and with it the stress
of fast technologies and global news. I begin listening
to silence, look at the flutters of yellowed birch leaves

and berry clusters already reddened on a rowan.
In a grassy clearing beeches line an ancient bank.
I press my hand against a scar and a cut that gapes

in a trunk, touch knuckling roots, try to absorb
the green of each ellipse of leaf and the oxygen
it's creating. A brimstone settles. Further in

I listen for rustles, look for the beams and tines
of antlers but no stag is standing motionless
in the shadow, no rabbit scurries into undergrowth.

A yew tree won't let me see into the muskiness
where its limbs huddle. When the path divides
I can't decide which trail to take, in the end choose

the one where a series of flat stones were laid
long ago. Poisonous fungi frill bark, damp seeps
into my bones. Brambles trip me, claw at my flesh.

I stare at the red rips, gasp as a bird squawks
and breaks upwards through twigs but the silence
reasserts itself. Now, I long for humans, for traffic whirr.

I try to run but giant trees have blocked my way,
stretched their arms across the sky – they'll strike
in this raven darkness. Suddenly lightning slits

the terrible stillness. Leaves shiver as if with fever,
joints creak. A crack and a tree falls crushing bracken
and saplings. Then the rushing that is rain. Drops

running down my face offer a release sweet as music.
Is it minutes or hours before I see turquoise drifting
above, hear a sound like shingle being dragged

by the tide from a sloping shore into a heavy sea?
Ahead is a track that's rutted and an unkempt cottage.
Bushes straggle across its windows, flowers

struggle in its garden where an old man is tipping
small stones from a wheelbarrow. I walk slowly
towards him to ask for directions. The forest follows.

MAESHOWE

Don't imagine entry is simple, a matter
of plunging in. Begin by following the path
between two fields. The closer you come
to the grassy mound the less you can utter

its power over you. Going in on your own
is not permitted. You're counted into a group,
stoop to follow the yellowish flicker along
a dark passage. Soon it dawns how alone

you are. You've never travelled so far back,
so far in. In the central chamber you watch
ovals from the torch glide over the masonry:
deftly placed slabs, buttresses, ridges stacked

high above your head. The small light shouts
the darkness and chill seeps into your body.
But a stillness that's other than death inhabits
this place where the undead gather to greet

the dead, where Vikings sheltered once
and left runes delicate as veined leaves,
where generations believed a hogboon lurked.
Long after you have gone away the sense

that spirit is housed in this tomb will remain.
In midwinter you'll visualize the sun piercing
the dark that swaddles seeds, see it falling
on the aligned entrance, its white shine

splitting to burnish the passage wall, flood
the ground with gold. In that deep chamber
you'll be bathed in red, not the red spilt in hatred –
the red that's birth, the heart blooming with blood.

Maeshowe: a Neolithic tomb on the mainland of the Orkneys
Hogboon: a mischievous spirit

HOTEL

ARRIVAL

'You can see she's innocent as snow – that nun
munching coleslaw sandwiches.' Eva isn't sure if Dan
spoke or if the words said themselves in her head.
Is this what she wants: to sit gorging on scones
above boats on a blue inlet while their bedroom
is being readied, to be held as if in a spell by a nun

in a frayed habit, a nun whose face is so white
it can rarely have been touched by unconfined air?
Saintly somehow, her quick plucking of an éclair
from the cakestand, her licking of melting chocolate
and the way she says meekly: 'So kind of you
to take me out,' to a lady in an overbearing hat.

The gratitude discomforts Eva and the terrace rails
glittering in the heat are making her head ache
but she runs down steep lawns past rosebeds,
past palms and pines, past *The Bluebell*
by the quay to the beach. The limpets clamped
to rocks and seaweed snaked across sand smell

of childhood. One dip in the sea – cold water
shocking the stomach, salt embracing shoulders
and she'll forget the stuff clogging her mind, forget
disasters in papers and politicians full of promises
like the pokes of pink sherbet she used to buy
as a child though she hated the sting in her throat.

Here, beauty is bedded and the affable porters,
the golf clubs, tennis racquets and striped umbrellas
in the vestibule give assurance of an ordered world.

Donkey-laden with their old rucksack and new
olive-green cases, a junior porter leads them through
lounges where elderly guests sip or snooze away

the afternoon among weeping cacti, past vases
of sweet-breathed lilies, up an elegant staircase, along
corridors to a dim room. Before supper they find
a library. Eva opens a bound novel – not a priceless
first edition though its pages are uncut. Glancing
at a locked window she's shaken by her faint face.

In the dining room a hundred white tablecloths
are doubled by mirrors and overhead countless drops
of light are suspended in glass. The head waiter,
whose cheeks record that he tipples, treats them
to banter, undoes serviettes fanned like peacock tails,
recommends the watercress soup and rack of lamb.

They're nibbling bones when a man in a mauve suit
passes with an entourage. A god from a Greek myth?
An ageing pop star who'll turn the hotel upside down
for a publicity stunt? Eva tenses. Surely not, it's miles
from anywhere. She must have peace, couldn't bear
racket tearing it to ribbons. As if she spoke, Dan smiles.

VIOLET

By the swimming pool in the sunken garden Eva
twiddles the crimped paper umbrella that adorned
her iced martini. Tired, though they've done so little,
she looks away from the water at passion flowers,
succulents, jasmine trailing from a trellis and feather-
headed grasses. A lady with silver hair appears,

two waiters in tow. One guides her by the elbow
to a nearby recliner, the other sets before her
a tray crowned with a plump china teapot. Eva
takes in her bird-patterned dress and piercing eyes,
is surprised to be addressed by an imperious voice:
'I've come here for forty years, I'm Violet Merrylees.

I suppose you're a newcomer?' Before she has time
to reply the old lady greets a well-preserved man
who kisses both her cheeks. His complacent face
suggests he's had a life of adulation and plenty.
Eva notices Dan's grinning. Later, in the bath, moments
from the day surface: trudging by yellowish fleece

edging a shore, over shingle tufted with heather, touching
fuschia gold, spying a heron that rose heavily from
a shrunken stream. After lunch they'd escaped the sun's
fixated eye in their room, shed clothes wildly which led
to sex which somehow she didn't enjoy. Before dinner
they watch the sunset. It's perfect, so is the squid

which she's eating when Violet, decked in turquoise
and sequins, is kissed by the head waiter and seated
at a central table. 'I can't wait to script a film here,'
Dan mutters. 'I'll work in that ancient mermaid
trying to lure sailors.' 'I thought we'd agreed
no talking about work this week.' The mauve slide

of blackberry mousse down Eva's throat smoothes
her irritation. After the meal she plumps for sitting
in the green lounge where there's a fire in the grate.
She queries the need for it as the porter pours
strong coffee into their fluted cups. 'Heatwave
or snow we light the fires every night of the year

in this room and the hall,' she's told. Hypnotized,
she stares at the logs' huge incandescent heart,
at the lick and leap of flames until she's distracted
by Violet's enthronement in a wing chair. The lights
are switched off and a cake with circles of lit candles
is wheeled in. Clapping. The head waiter recites

a poem to the birthday queen and, voice furred, leads
cheers for her eighty-fifth birthday. Sheepish singing
gives way to an Irish harp that's playing in the great hall.
Violet's elated by the attention, munches a slice of cake
and mouths to guests but Eva recognizes her loneliness –
knows she's sealed in a glass bubble she can't break.

THE ISLAND

Mid-morning and sultry as they walk past willowfields,
past willowherb taller than themselves edging
a ditch, gaze at fingers of land interleaving islands
rounded as whale backs rising from the silent sea.
Dan points at the smallest: 'I gather that belongs
to a hermit-like millionaire who comes and stays

for months every summer.' Eva imagines herself
drifting for days into water's changing blues, watching
butterflies with mosaics on their wings alight on gorse,
imagines weeks away from tiresome meetings, deadlines,
e-mails demanding instant answers and from being stuck
in the limbo of the Underground on a rush-hour train.

Following a path up the rivermouth they reach small islands
linked by bridges with wickerwork sides, listen to the pitter

of unseen insects. 'This could be a dream,' Eva murmurs
as they step onto an islet which leads nowhere. It offers shade
beneath waxy-leaved rhododendrons. Dazed by knots
in the branches, she closes her eyes but Violet invades.

She tries to shake off the summoning face but it sticks
like a burr and she pictures herself aged, feeding
on memories in hotel rooms, thinks of the courage
it requires to take a holiday in the past and quite alone,
is sorry she was irritated by a woman of such character.
Why not interview her? Her stories would be a goldmine

and she'd love to be photographed in the hotel. Even
in this idyllic place you can't forget you're a journalist –
don't you want more than that? Eva snaps at herself.
'Why the sigh?' Dan pats her arm. She shakes her head:
'I was in a trance.' He slips down her T-shirt strap,
'You're lovely today, come further into the wood.

The leaflet says rhododendrons strangle other plants
but I'm sure they don't touch people!' He kisses her neck.
How Gothic, Eva thinks, and sexier than our room –
the smell of twigs and leaf layers and dusky heat
rubbing against us. She feels connected to Dan,
his everywhere hands. They climax pouring sweat.

When they've eaten triangular sandwiches and fruit
immaculately wrapped by the hotel they lie down
on *The Times*. In moments Dan's snoring. Eva thinks
of the nun's habit as she sees a darkness stirring
in the branches. Nothing's there. She closes her eyes
but now she can hear the sound of a creature crying

in a pocket. On hands and knees she scrabbles
to find it, unearths an egg that's cracked. Shocked,
she watches liquid dripping from the fractured shell,
seeping into the ground. Grief overwhelms her but tears
bring no relief. Suddenly Dan's shaking her shoulder:
'Lightning's shooting over the water – it's going to pour.'

THE RUIN

'Golfing in paradise is what books call this course,'
says Patrick. For forty years he was head porter
at the hotel. Now he takes guests on guided walks.
He points his stick at the turf, at sleeves of trees
through which can be seen a postcard-blue sea,
at the line of hills rising against a flawless sky.

'Yes, we get all the champions here,' he chuckles. Eva
remembers catching snatches of Violet at breakfast
boasting about her husband, his shelves of silver cups.
Interviewing her would be utterly boring. She kills
the idea. Better a feature on Patrick, a talker who knows
how to spin out an anecdote as they climb to get a view.

Beneath is laid out a stunning series of peninsulas,
their hotel lording the smallest, and in the far distance
a coast so faint it could be easily be a hallucination.
Eva looks at the river uncoiling into the sea with its flock
of islands, longs to stay for hours in total silence
but Patrick offers his binoculars, points out a speck

in the water that's an outcrop of rock where seals
and seabirds breed. Then he plunges into the tragedy
of a skipper who took his boat across the bay

ignoring all warnings of severe weather, the fear
the watchers felt when it was driven off course,
then gobbled by waves just as the lifeboat drew near

and how the skipper's retrieved body was still warm.
Gazing at a sail on the motionless surface, Eva thinks:
a painted ship upon a painted ocean. Subdued,
the small group descend the hill, enter a pine wood,
come to a ruined castle that's a romantic frame
for shrubs, flower borders and waterspouts played

through sculpted fish mouths into stone basins.
Eva's struck by a kitchen fireplace with a tiled grate
and broad chimney that looks oddly vulnerable
in the middle of a wall beside a new-mown lawn.
She questions Patrick. 'Burnt down in a terrible fire –
the story is it was deliberately started.' The frowns

and smiles crossing Dan's face tell her he's deep
into a plot for yet another film and she wants to scream:
what about the fireplace's script, the uncontrollable roar
of heat, the bodies that burnt in this now-Eden, you fool?
She shudders as a peacock screeches in the creepery
on top of an urn. What about the reality within these walls?

THE SEAL

'Let's take brandies onto the terrace, escape all this,'
Eva scowls at the fiddlers playing non-stop in the hall,
at the clapping, singing and frothing beer. Outside,
Dan mutters: 'Our last evening. Will you ever forget
this beautiful place, the dramas lurking in its corners?'
Tigerlily and jasmine scent lie on layers of cooling heat.

Eva doesn't reply, lets him wonder if she's sulking
as they descend the gardens. Earlier they spent
hours on the shore where they prodded a lobster's
discarded leather, paddled, collected conical shells
but they're drawn to it again as the dusk moves in
like a silent bird and a huge amber moon swells.

At the top of the shingle they watch the indigo sea
rising and falling like even breath and fishing boats
gliding across the horizon like fireflies. Eva sighs,
aware of a longing to unlock. 'What's bitten you?'
Dan asks. 'Anyone would think a ghost put a curse
on you at that castle.' 'For all I know it did. Don't you see

one only has to scratch the surface of this idyllic place
to find a library of books with uncut pages, loneliness
that eveningfuls of people can't staunch, rhododendrons
snatching light and sap from other plants, waters
which drown, stones that watched bodies burning?'
'Eva, do Edens exist except as figments of matter

we create in our imaginations? Is paradise peacocks
flaunting in a garden or love beneath a leaking roof,
a bouquet of red roses or an insight in a steamed-up bus?
This is one thread in a plot that's running through my head.'
She nods, remembers an ocean shifting and shifting
in her sleep last night, refusing to rest in its bed

and a voice which kept repeating: *a white moon
drowning in a green sea*. She clutches Dan's hand:
'Look, a seal on that rock.' Gazing at the dark body,
its completeness, she has a sense of sliding, is freed
from she knows not what. She wishes she could see
the creature's human expression but it's too late, day

is draining fast. And it doesn't matter for the magic
of this creature, which legends say is able to shed
its skin on land and live as a person, has reached her.
Tonight, in bed she'll tell Dan she's not taken the pill
since they came here, won't mention that the weight
of his wanting was the reason. She begins to feel

longing herself. The seal moves. It's standing up.
Maybe it's the childlike nun – no, it's a man walking
up the beach with a fishing rod. Yet the vision lingers
as if the figure on the rock was a benign spirit that lives
beneath the willowfields and the islands, in the river
and the inlet. She'll go home with it planted inside her.

Note: *a white moon drowning in a green sea* is from 'Hen Felin'
by Grevel Lindop from *Playing with Fire* (Carcanet, 2006)

TO GO AWAY

is to unplug busyness, lock up routine,
travel for eight hours, arrive at
the Grand Hôtel des Bains and unpack
in a bedroom without a soupçon of trend

but with four doors and French windows
that could feature in a Feydau farce; is to recline
in the lounge sipping the transparent gold
of milkless tea and history's grandeur.

Being away is to stroll down to the river
which cuts through the town, is to gorge
on its ambered browns and mineral greens,
is to be immersed in its gushing voice

as it rushes over the weir and parts into tails
that drift sideways like the threads of ideas
which refuse to connect; is to follow
the white gabble at stones in the riverbed.

Being away is to peer into the spa centre
where the overweight, swathed in white towels,
wander through steamy heat in the hope
of trapping beauty. Away is ambling under planes

whose dappled trunks are reminders of the pelts
of grazing animals, is sitting with black coffee
on a café terrace reading Mansfield Park,
savouring its out-of-place Englishness.

*

Away, I wait for the Source Intermittente
in le parc. It wells quietly from dry stones,
rises almost to tree tops and the topple
is whiter than swansdown, flock, seedclock.

After two minutes it droops, recovers,
fizzles to nothing. But its sulphurs
simmer within the earth whose boilings
and coolings we can't alter, can't predict.

And every six hours it resurges as if to prove
to a circle of expectant watchers poised
with cameras that dramatic patterns occur
in a universe some insist is random.

THE MNAJDRA TEMPLES

As if they'd been thrown down by a god in a temper
rocks lie at random all over the hill. The ground
is riddled with stones. It ought to be barren

but it's given birth to flocks of yellow flowers
so jubilant they'd dull toucan beaks, to blooms
with crimson throats and minute un-English pansy faces.

I try to picture hunks of rock like these being lugged
and hewn five thousand years ago, the labour
of raising great buildings with apertures and domes

offered to the sky. Even lopped and crumbling,
their grandeur remains: a deep doorway intact
in a wall whose slabs still fit perfectly, a monolith

that's still striving upwards, rounded apses,
this solid spine of plant carvings supporting
an altar table. I think of the small figures

now in the museum, their huge elbows, their bellies,
hips and knees which so graphically celebrate
fecundity. The booklet is a mine of information

about oracular rooms, sacrificing oxen, the carrying
of food and drink in exquisitely shaped jars
through curtained chambers but it doesn't reveal

what the humans who worshipped here thought,
nor when nor how the human brain began making
complex plans, conceiving deities, temples.

It doesn't explain why this slope I'm standing on
is clad in so many colours – a treeless Eden.
I marvel at the easy drop into the unnameable blue

of a sea cloudless as the sky, a blue that shivers
down my backbone, a blue inhabited only
by a green-knobbed island with sides so sheer

it's safe from human landing, by a pale strip
on the horizon which might be a fishing boat
or simply a slip of the imagination. I read a note

about a nearby cave where archaeologists found
the fossilized bones of hippopotamuses, elephants
and long-extinct animals which roamed the hill

for millennia before the building of temples began.
And I see how small our tall technologies are,
see that our lives are hardly more than the flickerings

of this giant butterfly that's just landed on stamens
laden with orange pollen. It stops long enough
to allow me to follow the deep black edgings

on wings which sweep up dramatically to points.
And what I want is to send away the waiting taxi
and stay here at the brink of time and timelessness.

GOING BACK

Still there: the long station with wooden roof fringes,
the iron posts and a platform running beside the quay
but no trains spilling bucket-and-spade families
who hurry for the steamer – only cars queueing on the pier.
The reek of hamburgers, which didn't exist then,
doesn't mask the decay. This station is a ghost.

Still there: the Clyde, its lochs limbs reaching into land
but Cardwell Bay's a turquoise marina. In my school-days
it was grey as the gunmetal battleships which brooded
on the drizzled Firth and in the dimness before that
it was mighty, ended in France. The Bay Hotel's paintless –
the town, thriving in the war, is bypassed now. Still there:

the esplanade and my beloved Kennedy Steps. Once more
I climb them. The hundred and twenty-one have shrunk
and are bitten at the edges. I laughed and quarrelled
on these flights, on icy mornings slithered to the front
for the school bus and sometimes at dusk I dawdled
with Peggy Miller, scared to explain my lateness home.

Golf Road is still there. It's shorter but at the same
steep twist. At the last turn I'm shocked to a standstill.
Who has magicked the golf course where sheep grazed
into a housing estate? On the corner of Divert Road,
in the correct place and with its garden walls still intact
but terraces now doll-sized, stands our house.

Not there: the sandpit where sister and I invented worlds,
only a garage. Upstairs no one's undone the bars across
my childhood windows. In tears, I peer at the frosted
glass doors still dividing dining room and lounge. The moors
beyond the house are mere humps, the fields below them,
their cows, carthorses, clovers, are lost to tarmac roads –

a place with no soul . . . I click my camera but when I leave
the present peels away. Grass overgrows concrete,
the Bay is wiped grey. Knotting skipping ropes across
window bars, sneaking whelks up the Kennedy steps,
squeezing through barbed wire into the thistle fields,
trudging silksand on the moors – these are still there.

ARRAN

1

To cycle round the island was to touch upon shore
after immaculate shore, was to smell wildness
rooted in moors, was the feat of completing a circle.

Father, who was a tower of knowledge, an absolute
whom we never questioned, had pored over maps,
divided the expedition into seven days. But one morning

he was challenged by the wind on a high pass.
Joyfully it swooped upon his cape and blew into
the waterproof until its heavy yellow ballooned,

annulled his frantic pedalling and in spite of his might
he began to roll back down the steep hill. Is memory
tricking me or did the bike and its rider levitate

for seconds like that winged horse I'd met in myth,
like the prophet Elijah lifting to heaven? Not seeing
any danger, sister and I laughed and laughed

at the drama of Father not in charge. We didn't know
he'd never gain the control he desired in the world,
that he'd end life enraged by his powerlessness.

No, we'd no inkling of this as we faced the air's
huge bluster and ferried the sky on our shoulders.
We were enveloped in the moment, its glory.

2

On the fifth day we found ourselves on a beach that lay
at the Atlantic's mercy, a beach which far outshone
our rock and shingle shores at the mouth of the Clyde.

I sank fingers into the yielding silk of sand, pulled
from its whiteness: whelk shells with holes
like emptied eyes which had once held living flesh,

the hard tents of limpets, a purple twin unhinged
from its brother. By the sea's edge I peered
at rubbery ribbons trapped in scum thick as fleece

while wave after wave raised its enormous voice,
broke, collapsed. And in the lull while I waited for
the next overwhelm of sound I stared at the ocean.

Its fogged blue, dense, weightless, without
end, was shocking, shrank parents, sister, me
to nothing. Yet I had never seen such beauty.

ROOM

Let in the piano and the metronome,
a sentinel that stood on the lid next to books
with hooked notes and tocked strict time.

Let in my surprise when I peered inside
the exposed body at pallid rows of hammers
and the taut strings needed to produce sound.

Let in those nights when my mother played
and the family's four voices rose with
Loch Lomond or *Daisy Daisy,* dissolved

into the gingerbrown table, the wide smile
of the clock and the darkness outside
which shelved down to rocks at the Firth's edge.

Let in afternoons when I was nine, hurrying
The Blue Danube across the keys, fingers
tripping on a difficult chord, mother too close,

rapping my knuckles: 'My worst pupil.'
Let in that self, sixteen, practising in a room
in Sussex, aching to perfect a Chopin waltz.

TWO

Shutting the door to cut out voices needling
each other downstairs and the waves of tension
they created, opening to beech trees
in the silent garden – this happened often.

The dove-grey trunks, their green layers
calmed my out-of-kilter body but I could never
stamp out bleakness from the north-
facing room too small for all my belongings.

Yet this cell was my place. Here I delved
into literature, fumbled longings into words
melodic as meadows, recited Keats' odes
to the mirror which always dimmed me.

Relive that evening I crept into bed,
a pre-menstrual sense of doom hung
like a mighty roller-blind above my head
and threatening to drop its weight at any minute.

Prickled flesh cocooned between cool sheets,
I read Charlotte Brontë's *Shirley*, melted self
into the heroine till mother pushed in,
knife-sharp: 'Get up, it's too early for bed.'

THREE

My music teacher's piano was black
as her velvety cuffs, as the glint in her eyes.
Its waxy candles leant towards me like she did.

Peace carpeted her room which was graced
with marigolds, pansies, cowslips, campion –
(flowers whose names my mother had taught me).

I was soothed by the way she sipped tea
from a bone china cup, savouring the taste
yet listening to the sounds my fingers were making.

Elbows had to be kept well up, arms
make gentle sideways movements and hands
must never perform jumps, never crash

on the sensitive keys. Smiling, she picked out
the four tunes Bach had laced together
with such cunning, helped me to make each tell.

FOUR

Edge into the kitchen one day in the June
I was seventeen, the world honeysuckled
as the garden until mother unexpectedly said:
'When you were six I learnt how to get pills

to put in your milk if the Germans succeeded
in invading Britain. Much better for you
and your little sister to go to sleep for ever,
than fall into the Nazis' hands.' Years later

I recognized she loved me – that last
smile, thornless as honeysuckle, days
before she died sitting on a chair listening
to a sonnet of Shakespeare's on cassette.

But then, louder than hands smashing
a discord on the piano, what I heard was:
my mother wished to kill me. I gazed at
the stained and rucked stuff of rage and fear

too ashamed to allow anyone see it.
And I tried to bury dismay that my life
might have been snatched before I'd found,
before I'd pressed the keys at the heart of it.

BOW HILL

There were days when I climbed above
the yews covering its great curve to turf
spattered with tormentil and rabbit droppings,
scrambled and crawled up chalky slithers
towards a sky specked with lark song;
days when I picnicked in the hollow
of Hengist or Horsa, those emptied tumuli
crowning the ridge, and conjured up a past
when the hill was peopled and battle cries
broke above the sheep baaing, arrows
flew in flocks, slaughter ripped and silenced;
days when I half-believed that I'd found
at the heart of the hill Keats' *temple of Delight*
or a burrow where I'd be quite safe
from the intolerable; days I gazed far
beyond West Stoke Clump at the green
and dun patchwork of the fields below,
their thumbnail farms, at the haze rising
from the sea's dazzle – this was the world
my English teacher said lay before me,
a world so glistening with all I longed for
I wept, for I knew I would never reach it.

And now, more than fifty years on
when I've travelled far, found much,
Bow Hill has suddenly surfaced again.
I'd no idea it was so embedded, so beloved.
In my path: a figure whose head is covered
with a cloth. 'Why are you treading on voices,
buried voices?' he asks and slips away.

Looking back, I see I've trodden on turf,
flinty earth, raised roots and a heap

of collapsed feathers. I peer at the ground trying
to figure out how one steps on a voice
because voice is not fixed to place
though it seems to cling like smell –
like the fierce pungency of the fox that once
slid past me on the hill, muzzle sly
and determined. I think how voice departs
with its owner and though, like body
and place, it can be correctly recorded
what stays alive is memory: sliding
on chalk trails, treading on birdpecked shells,
finding a hare that's crumbling into earth,
the sudden lift of a bird into the blue,
all the voices planted inside the head.

STRAWBERRIES

1

After the wild strawberry seeds sprouted
in a cupboard's warmth I coddled the spider stems
on a windowsill until I thought they could cope
with the garden where the unpredictable hums.
Now, revelling in freedom, they're multiplying

delicately serrated leaves up and down
my borders and opening hundreds of white-
petalled flowers whose firm centres
promise a summer of small pink fruits
with pitted skins. Kneeling on the path

I'm twenty again, confused and intense,
searching under flowering currant bushes,
parting creeping violets from strawberry clumps.
As I watch myself peer into sun-grained rushes
of duskiness I come upon that moment

when the troubled, Crusade-weary knight
in Bergman's *Seventh Seal* who's on a trail
to unravel meanings, rises from sleep
and, as he sits on the grass drinking the cool
of morning, is offered a bowl of strawberries

by the young wife in a travelling troupe.
It matters not that the film's in black and white –
what I take in is the girl's flaxen hair, moist
meadow green, the pink fragrance of the fruit,
a world healing as dock leaves laid on a wound.

2

It's May and the hedge parsley bordering the stream
in the park stands as tall as myself. I don't want
to dip into its dream layers but the decades
drop away and I'm cycling by verges pent
with white to the nursery where it took a week

to plant out the young strawberries, put up
cloches – tedious work. And for once
the wind isn't blowing in from the salt and sand
of the sea but out of the blue it pounces
on dozens of glistening lids, ferries them

across the field, then lets its victims go.
They crash onto unbroken glass, shatter.
The slow afternoon ripped, we line up, shaken,
by the unharmed greenhouse and stare at the clutter
of frames, the crushed fruit, the speckless sky.

Seven years later the shock that struck
from the blue was greater. Late on the last day
in Rome with my new husband, I read on a board
'Kennedy Assassinata.' As if the ground below
my feet was no longer reliable I began to tremble.

This May I touch the unfathomable grasses,
nurture these small berries and, in the hope
of gathering ripe cupfuls in July, I pull off
the snails clinging to stalks. Often I pick up
the word *safe*, ponder its precise meaning.

SUMMER

1

Now is the time that saffron flowers flare
from courgette plants, the males on thin stalks,
the females tailed to small swellings. And here
beneath hairy umbrellas, ready to be picked,
solid as a baby's head, magical as moon:
a yellow globe on the rain-sweetened ground.
I turn to stare at the glittering white stone
of a block a mile away. My prize in my hands,
I imagine those who hatched and hid bombs
in one of its flats – the hate. Stunned, I sit
by the oregano that's run wild in a bed
of feverfew, fennel, compressed sunflower heads
where butterflies hover, bees hum as they sate
themselves on nectar, where nothing is numb.

2

Trapped in a train that reeks of sweat I spy
buddleia bushes blooming on gravelly ground:
a thousand purple plumes lifted to the blue
of a sky so clear it should unlatch my mind
from daily sirens and helicopter hum.
But I keep glancing at a man whose case,
lashed to a crate, might be a nest for a bomb.
I wish myself back to a hill, the space
above it wheeled by seabirds which alight
on glitters of mud at the edge of Scapa Flow.
In the grass at my feet: clover, crane's-bill,
cuckoo flower. I'm in Eden until we slow
and halt at a mud-grey station. The man hauls
his luggage off the train, limps to the exit.

FISHFACE

Sudden guffaws and obscenities jerk me from
a paragraph about crabs – their two pincers
and four sets of legs – to be confronted by
denims on the seat beside me. They end in trainers
with massive soles and studs stamped on the uppers.

As we rush along a woman in a charcoal suit
hisses in acid classroom at the owners, two lads
in hoods: 'Take your feet off the seats.'
'Is she living in this century, off her head?'
The four of us are alone in the long compartment.

The taller boy leans over the pursed face,
grins, grabs it by the chin. Should I try and pull
the taut cord? 'What did you say, cunt?'
The chin's waggled. A crack now in her shell.
Heart bumping, I expect a knife – her blood, mine.

At Bounds Green the aggressor releases the chin.
Shouting, the pair slouch down the platform.
At last we move on and I hear myself spilling
words of sympathy. Her answer's a curt nod.
I'm absorbing the tucks in her blouse and the chill

she's created when she becomes a fish I saw
in the aquarium in Orkney, its round stare,
downturned mouth and how it flicked away
as if to avoid contact. But pearly glints
patterned its sinuous body and it lured me

into a waterworld where I was shown
through a magnifying glass newborn lobsters
no more than minute strands of weed,

a large eel wriggling into gravel, a scallop
whose hard fans clacked as it jumped. And hiding

its vulnerable flesh under a stone was a crab
waiting for a new carapace tough as the red
leathery case nearby that it had recently shed.
The keeper knew each creature in his care,
checked daily on its health and mood,

addressed it by name. As the cold face recalls me
I remind myself that sea-animals show cruelty
but the motives for human savagery gather,
beat in my brain. At Arnos Grove I escape
the train, climb steps to the blue weather.

THE CAT IN THE BAG

On a traffic island in suburbia
it dawns on me I've mislaid my bag,
the bag bulging with everything I need to function,
the capacious bag in which I've tucked my profound possessions.

I need to sweeten my house
for the very important person who's decided
to pay me a visit but without the bag I can't get inside
and I'm on the verge of slipping down the long birdneck of panic.

But look, by my feet, my cat!
Comforting to stroke her white bib, feel
the rise and fall of her purring fur. A rockweight
falls off my back for I remember I put my beloved in the bag

on my way out. If she's turned up
the bag must be nearby. No sign of it –
not even on the tarmac squashed to a skin by tyres.
And now the cat has vanished into the ache that's everywhere.

Here is my best friend's flat.
She's in her kitchen dwarfed by towers
of plates, threatened by cutlery. If I help her surely
she'll let me use her phone to report my worrying loss? But already

her patience is beginning to ebb
and my hope of dialling the police station,
re-entering the house, picking up my dirty socks
and making a bed for the important personage, falls apart.

I sidle out and down the steps
to the pavement. The vicious sun follows me
all the way down the road. I need my protective glasses
but they're folded up in their case in the lost bag, doubly blind.

And now I'm trying to work out
why I stuffed the cat into a bag to suffer
credit cards poking from pockets I've never plumbed
and no compartment wide enough for my precious, my pearl.

Did the comb's teeth dig
into her ribs as I zipped up, cutting off
her source of air. Somehow she must have managed
to wriggle out – or did I clasp a mirage in the middle of the street?

Forget the plastic cards, forget
preparing the house for the personage. Unless
I find the one who never claws, who never refuses love,
my sadness will be a sack weighted with stones and I'll drown.

JOURNEY

I thought I'd scotched the exam dream by writing it down
but it's sneaked back. As I wake up I ask myself
why I've dreamt failure again. And now,
trapped on a bus that's overpacked with children
newly fledged from school, with women
yoked to shopping, with pushchairs and irritability,
I ask again: why has someone thrown away
their life on the Piccadilly Line? And I'm appalled
at the unending blankness the person must have seen,
don't want to enter it. Even the black rows of seat backs
speak despair. Why? I ask and this time I'm crying
and remembering how I slowly cast off fears which clung
like Cinderella rags, remembering the love I've been given.
Outside, I glimpse a heap of oranges, each a small sun,
and stares from uncurtained windows. We lurch
to a standstill thirty yards from a stop. An elderly
Indian man in a hat with earflaps shouts at the driver
to open up. The driver roars back. Muttering breaks out
like a measles rash. I can smell the bodies underneath
coats – any minute now the anger will fizz over. At last
the doors of this glass and metal trap zip apart
and what I want is to stream out with the overladen,
the crumbling, the long-legged kids in their clunky shoes.
What I want is to walk along Green Lanes in nothing
but the simple cool of my skin past the unending,
unbeautiful buildings, past the rows of steel kisses
sealing the entrances to Underground Stations.
What I want is to say: praise be for the wren I saw
this morning among the tiny flowers blue-creepering
a terrace wall, for the scrawled notes in my bag,
for mobile phones which offer the chance to send
urgent messages, praise be for Sioux Talbot,

who I read about in a magazine, how she abandoned
middle age in Bournemouth to open an orphanage
in Kathmandu because its streets are full of children
who have lost their parents. What I want is for politicians
to apply their naked minds to this planet's destitution.
What I want is for grassless Green Lanes to continue.

NOTHING

Rain cracks, blears the compartment windows.
Outside: the dun of furrowed fields and for miles
November grass greying in hollows and humps,
seeping into lightlessness. Goosedown mist
hovers beneath the heavy-bellied sky.

Suddenly huge wings veer across clouds
above a sea the wind's worked up. I watch
waves spluttering against a jetty's spindle legs
until the train careers into the dark of nether hell.
We emerge to see chalky walls and I'm riding

back to a time when I was drawn to a precipice
where a terror I couldn't see, couldn't name
threatened to push me into the abyss of insanity
or nothing's stab. How face nothing? I ask now
but shrink from looking at the void which will caress

for ever. Later, in the bird sanctuary, nothingness
reveals its beauty: the precise but vacant cradle
of delicate bones that was once a bird's head,
a shell's patterned whorl, the dauntless stare
from a stuffed owl, and lying on brilliant grass

the skin a corn snake has shed. It's pale as grief.
No sign at first of the snake in the glass tank
but then, rippling yellow and black, it rises
from gravel, gravel that holds minute nothings,
seeds that will crack, eggs that will hatch – life.

BLAKENEY

Land is king here. The sea struggles
to keep its waterways between marsh and field.
In the harbour at low tide water dribbles
over sandbars and in the shallows gulls stand
on their doubles. The path to the coast is bone dry.
I love the miles of reeds straight as seabird legs.
They flame to orange where they've found moisture.
Skyblue pools succeed among grasses,
among glasswort clumps thronged by warblers.
And what is it I want – that pale strip
pulling me like a magnet, the unhookable sea
with ever-shifting glitter, the chance of slipping
from everyday clutter, wading in, undoing
flesh and letting the self loose in everness?

STILLNESS

1

Water is never completely motionless –
even the calmest lake stirs and laps
or prickles in wind. Stones are different. Massed
on beaches their gravity suggests they've kept
vigil for centuries; embedded in the ground
they seem to have slept soundly since Earth began
in spite of signs that they've been hurled, pounded,
compressed, expelled. This smooth pebble of mine,
its face painted with Port Isaac Bay,
pictures on the back its long ago distress:
greyish pools mottled with white and mapped
with dark continents. But there are days
when I contemplate the self-sufficient shapes
of stones and long to possess their stillness.

2

In darkness let your fan of fingers open,
imagine amethyst's purple crystals
at a geode's heart liquifying to honey
until your face muscles loosen, your shoulders,
which have borne so much, begin to unlock
and stillness is a quilt over your body,
a feather lining within. Now the tock
of pulse emerges and breath passes quietly
as a slippered friend. Beyond the house tyres
whirr on tarmac and geese call as they rush
the sky. The grief of the bereaved will push
into your room and nameless losses sustained
by the displaced. Hold silence and you may hear
rain on fruitless fields, grasses rising again.

MILK BOTTLE

Rinse one and you'll be rewarded with a winking lacery,
     spherical gas masses:
globe balanced on ballooned globe,
     floating fragilities,
each begging to inhabit the imagination.

Precise chambers with slanting walls come to a point
     in the bottle's depths.
Their curved roofs cling together, make
     the structures definitive
as cut glass, insubstantial as castles in the air.

And these architectures shift, could be beings
     poised like ourselves
on the edge of tremor. But they don't have aspirations,
     attitudes, passions,
don't carry spiritual beliefs, a fear of death.

Soon they'll collapse or explode in silence
     and nothing will remain
but a bottle in the sink, a sill with a cracked tile,
     darkening windows. Don't
weep because you can't re-create this weightless now.
     Enter and exult in it.

GOULASH

for Grevel

A crucial ingredient is the right frame of mind
so abandon all ideas of getting on. Stop pedalling,
dismount, go indoors and give yourself masses of time.
Then begin by heating a pool of oil in a frying pan
and, Mrs Beeton style, take a dozen onions
even though the space you're working in is smaller
than the scullery in a Victorian mansion. Pull off
the papery wrappings and feel the shiny globes' solidity
before you chop. Fry the segments in three batches.
Don't fuss about weeping eyes, with a wooden spoon
ease the pieces as they turn translucent and gold.
When you've browned but not burnt the cubes of beef
marry meat and onions in a deep pan, bless the mixture
with stock, spoonfuls of paprika, tomato purée
and crushed garlic. Enjoy the Pompeian-red warmth.
Outside, the sun is reddening the pale afternoon
and you'll watch as it sinks behind blurring roofs,
the raised arms of trees, the intrepid viaduct.
In the kitchen's triumph of colour and light the meat
is softening and everything in the pot is seeping
into everything else. By now you're thinking of love:
the merging which bodies long for, the merging
that's more than body. While you're stirring the stew
it dawns on you how much you need darkness.
It lives in the underskirts of thickets where sealed buds
coddle green, where butterflies folded in hibernation,
could be crumpled leaves. It lives in the sky that carries
a deep sense of blue and a thin boat of moon angled
as if it's rocking. It lives in the silent larder and upstairs
in the airing cupboard where a padded heart pumps
heat, in the well of bed where humans lace together.

Time to savour all this as the simmering continues,
as you lay the table and place at its centre a small jug
in which you've put three tentative roses and sprigs
of rosemary. At last you will sit down with friends
and ladle the dark red goulash onto plates bearing
beds of snow-white rice. As you eat the talk will be bright
as the garnets round your neck, as those buried
with an Anglo-Saxon king in a ship at Sutton Hoo,
and the ring of words will carry far into the night.

LARDER

MARGARET

The word's a misnomer for this kitchen cupboard
with wooden shelves hidden by creased fablon, with vents
that admit air from our London garden and far beyond.

Our so-called larder stores no coolth – how could it,
wedded to a wall facing south onto a terrace that mimics
Africa when summer bursts out? Real larders, like the one

in your house, Margaret, have marble shelves, walls thick
as the length of an arm, a shaded window. It takes seconds
to step back decades and lift the muslin cover

from the wide-lipped jug. Your house echoed the larder:
passages with overflowing bookcases, a roomy kitchen,
the comforting quiet of lounge sofas – a quiet that grew

from you. Ginger-haired, wide-hipped and flat-faced,
you weren't outwardly beautiful but pale girls
who were shut up in borstals would run to hug you

whenever you visited. You were beautiful to them,
to me too when my teens ended and, lost in the world,
I failed my parents' expectations. Dear Margaret,

you who cupboarded such kindness, offered me
a refuge from judgement. And yet you told me in old age
you had always felt yourself to be a misfit in the world.

THE AMALFI DISH

It dwells on our larder's top shelf, dwarfs
the tuna tins and torn seed packets
that still carry unplanted seeds.
Wide enough to diminish dinner plates,
it dips in fluted curves from a scalloped rim.
On its surface fanciful blue leaves trumpet,
oranges and lemons sing, balloons bloom
on strings.
            Nothing was bright the day
we went to Amalfi – no dreamblue sky,
no sun making love to the sides of cliffs,
neither oranges nor lemons nested among
branches. Clouds, heavy as winter coats,
hung over the town, rain spat as we neared
the shore, the sea wasn't calm as porcelain.
Its restlessness warned it was in a temper
and we hurried away, found grand steps
to the church which was as dim as doom.
Only the ceramics shop offered colour –
counter, shelf and wall, begged us
to buy. We chose a dish, bore it away.

On the bus overpacked with tourists and locals
I clutched our trophy as we braved the pelt
of rain and followed the road beside the precipice,
as traffic pinned us at hairpin bends, clutched it
as lightning forked and a German student
wiped the driver's steamed-up windows
while he tried to inch the vehicle past a coach,
clutched it as I glimpsed a cliff drop
which was surely greater than any

Dante faced when he traversed from circle
to circle in nether hell. One slip and the bus,
the dish, all of us would shatter on rocks
in the sea below. At last we achieved Sorrento
and everyone burst into applause for the driver,
for the joy of being alive.
                    Now, in the silence
of the larder the dish holds oranges, apples
and a day that still glints like a dark plum.

PAULA'S BOWL

for Erwin and in memory of Paula Schneider, my mother-in-law

The higgle of packets, purple-lidded canisters of pasta,
pumpkin seeds, oatcakes and the tiger-faced biscuit tin
on the larder's lowest shelf are queened by the large bowl

Paula made. With its unsymmetric sides, a leafy pattern
on earthbrown and bright yellow trunks, it's cousin
to bowls in Matisse paintings, carries the kiss of Picasso

and our daily bread. If Paula had seen the muddle
around it – she who brought imagination and practicality
to every shelf, wall and cranny of her house in Stamford Hill –

she'd have bubbled with ideas for transforming the larder
and our home, built the extension we'd half-envisaged
but shied away from. What she couldn't mould was her own life.

The bowl goes deep but not deep enough to hold everything
she lost: her art school place under Kokoschska – in 1919
life in Vienna was as insecure as skating on thin ice;

the portfolio of paintings she once showed to her children –
orange women with arms flung out, meadows glorious
with flowers and grasses; her home; her parents and sister

when she fled from Hitler to England. The large bowl,
its mazurka leaves, insect-dot blossom, tell how she felt
as a potter but the cool of the varnished interior

remains silent as sealed lips – refuses to whisper
her sharp disappointment that so little of her work sold.
In our house terracotta children in bell skirts are dancing

round a maypole. Blue florets speckle the long white dress
of a figure sitting on the ground, candleholders flower
on her head, hands, outstretched feet. A finger-thin dog

sniffs at a mottled triangular plate. Here, she's still alive
but every time I take bread from her bowl I remember
what was given, what was snatched out of her reach.

CAKE TINS

for Ben

Our larder floor is a subworld in which darkness
is relieved by occasional gusts of light. It boasts
an oblong of mottled lino that's lasted fifty years.
Between the rack, where elderly potatoes
are putting out white feelers, and a bottle
of extra virgin oil whose neck gleams
with olive gold, is the tier of circular tins
for storing cakes, each topped with a yellow lid.
What's happened to time? Once I had enough

to bake Victoria sponges, press them together
with raspberry jam, to make a ceremony of stirring
a fruit cake, not minding the blister
the spoon dug into my hand. I remember
Ben at five, pouring all his energy
into helping, his concentration as he cracked
an egg on the bowl's rim, the perfect yolk
landing on the table in a transparent pool.
All the years he ate cakes and casseroles
with gusto, I quite failed to notice
how thoroughly he was digesting the contents
of cookery books. Now, he serves us sea bass
with a beurre blanc sauce, chocolate torte . . .
Today when I sit at the kitchen table
and read the words crying from the paper
I see no point in cooking a gourmet meal
or stirring the bowl in which stewed tea
has been seeping all through the night
into raisins, sultanas and treacly sugar.
Yet the scent of fermentation is as potent
as the moment that scrawl kneads into dough
for a poem, as every coming together
so I add an egg and mix – for what is life
if it isn't a series of small makings
to stack up in larders against death?

MUD

Why did I wake this morning
remembering a day decades ago
when we drove up the spine
of England to the Harringtons' house
in a once industrial village to the north
of Durham and how the two boys,
theirs and ours, were uncooped
into the slate of late afternoon
with warnings not to do
anything foolish? In half an hour
the pair reappeared clad in mud
from armpits to toes. Buttoning
laughter behind stern words,
we peeled off the slimed clothes,
threw them into buckets
and dumped the boys in the bath.
After two soapings which left
a richly chocolate sediment,
the children emerged penitent
and pink as newly-hosed piglets.

This mid-March morning
the air from the window's so cold
it makes me think of a line of stiff
overnight washing as I lie
trying to unravel lines of thought,
so why do I suddenly become
a hippopotamus wading into
Kipling's great greasy
Limpopo River? Why do I ignore
the likelihood of crocodile jaws

and submerge in thick brown waters
where mangroves tangle, my snout
just above the pungent surface?

The questions sink into
a cool and rippling slowness,
melt among the fine hairs of weeds
and for a few minutes I forget
that the world's rivers, its arteries –
are drying up. Heaving my bulk
onto the bank, I roll myself in silt
until my back's coated in a mess
of silk. The sun's savagery softens,
laughter trickles through my body.

SISTER KENNEDY

A tank, she charged firing: 'I won't have men
in the ward at night,' overrode the doctor's note
granting permission. In seconds *my man* was outside

the swing doors, his bewildered face glinting
and pressed to small panes. I signed to him: phone
and complain. Like a goldfish he opened his mouth

but she blocked him out with swift curtains
and flung back the sheet. 'Part your legs,'
she rapped. 'There won't be a baby tonight,

when labour starts, you'll *know*.' I wanted
to pack words with mockery and hit back.
Instead, I lay helpless under my stomach's mound.

In the morning nurses smiled and *she* receded
like a bad dream. My man was present, yelped
with excitement, wept when the baby burst

into the world in the nick of time – minutes before
night shift began. Bundled out, he passed
Sister Kennedy in the corridor ready for battle.

In maternity I believed I'd escaped her.
Two days later, womb sore, head a thick blanket,
I dared to pick the baby up and for the first time

I felt he belonged to me, was proud. As I placed him
on the bed *she* descended: 'Germs on the quilt,
move that infant. Clearly you don't know a thing

about babies.' Her voice crushed the first bud
of confidence although I knew why she'd attacked:
her face was a battered pan, her waist weighty,

her backbone rigid as the routines she'd established
and she had to endure new babies, new mothers
who'd been touched with passion and entered –

she who'd never been unlaced by loving hands,
whose womb was an unused sack. I understood
she couldn't bear sympathy. Her fruit was bitterness.

THE GIRL IN THE CHAGALL MUSEUM

Why is she sitting so small and tightly closed?
Nine at most, her stillness compels, wrests
attention from Jacob on the ladder wrestling with dream.

Curled over the sheaf of white papers on her lap,
mice fingers on row after row of raised dots,
she's marooned in this temple dedicated to sight.

Is she reading about Jacob's braced mauve back,
the silver lick illuminating his knee muscles? Is mauve
to her the honeyed scent of buddleia, tasting brambles?

Angels billow, midnight blues and sensual reds leap
from the walls. They don't hide her fluent fingers
or wipe the sticky soreness of her half-shut eyes.

Now she's being guided towards Adam and Eve,
Chagall lovers relaxed among lighthearted bouquets
and woolly animals. She's placed at a hand's width

from the wolf, must be looking at its plum pelt
with peripheral vision. Can she see the crouched lion,
the green prancing in the garden? Abruptly she turns away.

Nearby the guilty pair run from the garden of paradise
to a world of wrongs. Below them at exactly her height
a purple fish is plunging, flippers spread like wings.

MARTHE

In the photograph the bath is white-sided, deep
as a tomb, the tiled walls are overbearing
and the patch of gleam reflecting the window

doesn't ease the claustrophobia. The wooden chair
with jutting uprights and crossbars is the one
her husband perched on to recreate his dream

of Marthe, muse, lover who's ageless whether naked
and splayed in sleep on a rumpled bed, pouring
water into a ewer or clothed in yellow at a table.

Invited into this small room we're close enough to touch
her skin, dip into her body's perfumes, can't help
prying into privacies: the bath's softened lips,

her button stomach, narrow hips, legs. But even
as we see she could slip like a fish from the tub's
lower end into nothingness, even as we feed

on the colour and light in which she's arrayed
for ever, we imagine the woman webbed with blood
filling the bathroom with dreams insubstantial

as steam, then wonder if her husband heard a stream
of shrill complaints, if she lay in silent thought
while water lapped or if her thoughts were bats

fluttering in obsessive circles. For all her visibility
she's vanished into the ghostly multitude of women
who've left no word behind, no trace of their voices.

EURYDICE'S VERSION

Of course, I was gobsmacked, weak at the knees
with joy to see beautiful you, your face radiating
adoration. Love rushed through me, a river

in flood. Yet even as I wept at the thought
of all the obstacles you'd overcome to reach me
I knew you'd won your way in not by bravery

but by charm. It didn't make a scrap of difference –
the hundreds of budding doubts about our relationship
were nipped and all I wanted was to be subsumed

in you. The silvered air that hung between us
was an intolerable curtain. Smiling sweetly,
and too knowingly, you lifted that lyre of yours

which no one can withstand. Surprise surprise,
the sounds were more melodic than the nightingale's,
more rhythmic than the bumblebee's humming –

hypnotic. Whimpering ghosts stopped
wandering, Tantalus forgot the branches
of red-cheeked peaches dangling just out of reach,

Sisyphus knelt on the boulder which drives him
and everyone else mad as he huffs it up that hill
only to watch it bounce down again and Hades

sat slumped on his throne. Even that brute
Cerberus stopped bristling. Eyes transfixed
in his three heads, ears pricked, tongues lolling,

he lay on the ground harmless as a newborn lamb
for over an hour. And I was your *thing* again,
my only desire to be reunited with you.

I could have scratched out Hades' eyes
for making you fill in a form, querying several
of your answers, laying down conditions.

When we finally left I was jubilant, trotted after you,
was eager to see day and smell grass, on fire
to lay my nakedness next to yours. But the moment

you turned round I was jerked out of my trance.
Your name seemed to shrivel even as I uttered it.
Passionless, I watched as you were driven

down that long passage and I didn't miss the way
you cried and kicked like a child in a tantrum
as you were hauled up to the world of light.

Oh yes, it was fantastic in the beginning –
being loved by the most famous musician
on earth, hearing you murmur I was the source

of your inspiration, watching timid deer raise
their antlered heads to listen to you playing,
swans snowy as innocence sailing

towards you, trees shaking all their leaves
in ecstasy. Tears swam into my eyes when women
left the wells where they were drawing water,

when farmers stopped harvesting and stood
open-mouthed in their fields, when mighty leaders
threw down their swords. A simply brought-up girl,

I could hardly believe a man with god-like powers
had chosen *me*. I worshipped the ground
you trod and if you touched me I all but fainted

into orgasm. Yet from the wedding day,
though I did my best to ignore it, something jarred.
The personage at the centre was you, the bride

was an adjunct to the ceremony, an object
decked in tiers of white, her china-doll face
hidden by veils, an idol smothered in flowers.

In the few months that we were married
my misgivings jelled and grew like an embryo
lodged in my womb. Whenever I was alone

the depressing weight dragged me down.
Ashamed, I tried to refuse it, squash, abort it.
If you get this message I bet you'll try and make out

I was brainwashed but I wasn't – and I need to set
the record straight about that shepherd, Aristaeus.
The story you put around is a complete fiction.

I was standing in the middle of a meadow
among poppies and pimpernels whose petals
hadn't been compelled to listen to your singing.

He wasn't a bit like you. Maybe he did fancy me
as I stood there in the grainy ripeness
gawping at flowers and humming to myself

but he didn't try anything on, didn't gush
about my beauty or whisper he wanted to sing
to me, write poems to my lips, paint my portrait,

none of that stuff – the opposite, in fact. I knew
he'd registered the *actual* me because he said:
'You look as sad as your singing sounds.'

And while his newly-clipped flock stood behind him
sniffing the summer air he looked at me
with such sympathy it was all I could do not to cry.

Oh yes, I took to my heels – you were right
about that – not because he attempted to seduce me
but because my heart was melted by his kindness,

because I recognized the truth in his words
but was too shocked to face it, because
I sensed this man could offer me a different life

and I was much too scared to grasp it.
I wiped him out of my mind as fast as I could
and was rushing back to you when the snake bit me –

a punishment maybe for throwing away happiness.
But, when, untrusting, you turned round to check
I was following you out of Hell the cord between us

was cut and the truth struck me like a force nine gale.
I went straight to Hades and thanked him
for proving it wasn't *me* you adored but a figure

you'd cooked up and perfected in your imagination,
that it was she you'd set apart and hymned
for hours on end though at the same time

you cast her as bedmaker, breadmaker, whore,
babymaker, milk-breast, childminder, nurse,
comforter, slave, mystic maiden, high goddess,

muse to be sucked forever for inspiration,
fool who existed only in relation to you,
a thin and pliant branch on your magnificent trunk.

Peeping into the passage of centuries to come
I saw your appalling creation being handed
down the generations. 'Fuck that!' I yelled

which made all those transparent souls
laugh until they wobbled like children's party jellies,
that beastly dog grin and the whole of hell

rock with mirth. Slowly I've come to value
this place. The living, for all they strut about
on the surface, fear the Underworld. I need

its darkness to see reality, to comprehend light.
In this kingdom I've learnt to listen, to think
for myself and when I speak I am heard.

THE MINCER

Fitting the handle to the twisting blades
of what might be stomach or heart, is a feat.

When it's fully assembled the heavy innards
can be viewed through the gape in the head.

A screw buttons the rings of the mouth. Once
the table's in its grasp, thanks to metal wings,

anyone can see the mincer is not to be messed with.
It's as familiar with holding back as the black dog

with two heads, has never heard of the country
of perhaps. Neither subtlety nor beauty

are words in its language – there are half a dozen
for mastication. I manage to avoid this character now

but once I saw it being packed on Wednesdays
with dry chunks cut from the Sunday roast

and watched it force out squiggles of meat
that were miserable as the drizzle at the window.

Every scrap was cut, every scraping saved.
Time was devoured by shelling, mincing, peeling.

Oh yes, the mincer, exhibiting its body parts,
lurked beneath the shiny surface of my childhood.

It meant hot red punishment dug into the palm
of the hand as the mulish handle resisted.

It meant becoming a woman was to be clamped
to kitchen, mangle and ironing board. It meant

the boredom of dusters, joylessness – and not
even a shelf for the self to bloom. It meant

lying in bed wishing irons to rust, dusters
to die, and promising myself I'd never mince.

THE RED DRESS

My first reaction is: I want it,
can't wait to squeeze into
a scarlet sheath that promises
breasts round as russet apples,
a waist pinched to a pencil,
hips that know the whole dictionary
of swaying, can't wait
to saunter down an August street
with every eye upon me.

But the moment I'm zipped in
I can't breathe and the fabric
hugging my stomach without mercy
pronounces me a frump.
Besides, in the internet café,
where you can phone Tangiers
or Thailand for almost nothing
fourteen pairs of eyes
are absorbed by screens.
No one whistles when I smile
at boxes of tired mangoes
and seedy broccoli heads
outside the Greek superstore.

By now I'm in a fever to undo
the garment and pull it off.
And for all its flaws, for all
that it only boasts one breast,
I'm overjoyed to re-possess
my body. I remember I hate
holding in and shutting away.
What I want is a dress easy
as a plump plum oozing

juice, as a warm afternoon
in late October creeping
its ambers and cinnamons into
leaves, a dress that reassures
there's no need to pretend,
a dress that's as capacious
as generosity, a dress that willingly
unbuttons and whispers in the ear:
be alive every minute of your life.

WALL

for Jennifer

1

This is a tentative world. Ahead the ground
rises, unrolls slowly into distance. Grass
straggles from sparse clumps. The only sound
is silence. On trees thin as bird legs: a fuss
of feathers. Maybe the smudged chimney and roof
are figments of imagination. But the wall
has a solidity which would support grief,
guides the walker and her dog up the hill,
reaches beyond the point eyes can see
into the future's opaque sky. The way
is planted with snares but they'll plod to its end
and the dog will linger to sniff the moment's petals,
the wall will shield the woman from the wind
as she hugs her thoughts, their jet darks, opals.

2

Not the wall of a stately English home,
aged yet reassuring with apple trees
espaliered across its bricks. Not the climb
of walls to ancient roofs whose towers praise
the blue of sky, not even a drystone wall,
the kind I grew up with on the moors above
the Clyde, the kind that spells pink bells,
grasses thin as peewit cries and troves
of marigold in marshwater. This is the wall
Hadrian built with blocks of stone to stop
marauders from the north. And yet it's more
than that: the unseen barrier we all build
to fend off hurt, the one we must leap
if we're to reach the pastures we long for.

FIELD

Once it was crossing the unmade road to sing
to wet mouths that chewed, stare at the sway
of udders soft as babies' heads, sniff milkiness,
glimpse emerald wings on cracked dung;

was nibbling the seeds in ripe heads of rye,
picking clovers – the pink and mealy white,
was thistles prickling legs and lying among feather-
head grasses that tickled as they brushed the sky;

was the night the carthorses raced round
driven by an electric storm's purple slashes,
their madness spilling into my excitement,
drops of light next morning glistening the ground;

was climbing the Downs, letting out the fears
penned in my head and walking a stubble field
to a blackened mill that stood defiant as it whirled
cloud and sun, roared its energy into my ears.

Now, field is the sweep below the spinney
in the park. Its glorious grasses stand unpawed
by city, smell of hay and are rarely mowed.
Here, carwhirr is muffled, collies plunge

into jungles of pungent stalks, tortoiseshells
flitter over ragwort. Ragged lines of geese
flap darkly across the setting sun's fleece
and utter warnings that day is paling out.

Here is fade, fall and rot till willows beginning
to green signal the white surprise of spring:
blossom on blackthorn knobbles, scatters of long-
winged anemones. And where dandelions hold up

their gorgeous yellow crowns, stinging nettles
herd and cunning spiders hang their threads,
where beetles scarper, slithery worms bed,
who knows what could sprout, run wild?

THIN WHITE GIRL

after 'To a Fat Lady Seen from a Train' by Frances Cornford

Oh why do you stride through the feathery grass,
hat pale as your hair and with back bared,
oh thin white girl, is it certainty of love
that makes you trample the park's green glory
now summer's unzipped? Whatever your story
why not sit in the cool and coo like a dove?

The fat white woman – have you come across her
clumping through fields imprisoned in gloves –
the one tartly accused of missing so much?
Maybe she longed to be naked and touch
buttercup gold, whiskers soft as love,
ached to kiss seedheads and nuzzle clover.

And who are we to smirk and preen as we rush
about town in cages on wheels or slouch
in parks without spotting heron or spotted thrush?
And where is the insect that was crawling the beach
of my beige page? It was red as my heart.
Oh why am I missing so much and so much?

SKYWARDS

A Chinese lad slender as bamboo
    is sitting in lotus position
        on the grass, palms turned up
           to receive a blue blessing

and a girl is worshipping the air
    by sweeping her arms over her head.
        I reach up to the coolness too,

see a crescent of moon flimsy
    as the tip of an idea tapping the brain.
        Dodging the sun that's conquered
           the east, I enter the small wood,

come to the hole where grainy light
    flows in and two tortoiseshells
        are darting through their hours of life.

Already berries redder than blood
    warn of the winter that is coming.
        But in the street beyond the park
           a new van stands by the kerb

and sky-dot-com is written large
    on its sides. When I see the ladder
        strapped to its roof I can't stop myself from

imagining unseen hands unfolding,
    raising, leaning it against the high
        sapphire wall, angels queueing
           to climb rungs and Jacob too stunned

to report the sighting. My fear
    of what lies ahead dissolves into slivers
        of moon, into bodies receiving the air.

DROUGHT

THE WATERING CAN

Eight in the morning – already the cool
is ebbing. The moon is a thumbprint
in the sky and in minutes the sun's all-
consuming smile will swallow the garden.

A sip of juice and I'm hurrying down
the terrace steps. In my left hand,
but only half full, is the pale green
watering can. I'm trying to balance

different demands: the cry for water
from plants unaware hoses are banned
with the whinings from my right shoulder
that it's not fit to pull its weight.

Perfect balance isn't possible, I decide,
looking at the clay. Sodden in May,
it's now dry as the belly of a riverbed
in Africa. Besides I can't bear to leave

feathery green leaves to wither,
to lose yellow flowers promising
clusters of fruit. I wish I could smother
the bullying light and extricate myself

from the heat wrapping itself round
my body which is limp as the pages
of the faded Penguin paperback I found
yesterday: *Paradise Lost*, with notes

I scribbled at University. Is it fear
of losing the green paradise of England,

fear it'll be brown for ever that's spurring
me to cart the can, or the need to prove

I have at least one practical skill? Spilling
water over the tomato plants, I pretend
I'm God releasing rain, not a fool.
Then I baptise white raspberry flowers.

THE BUDDLEIA

is losing its struggle to survive. Wizened arms
hold out baby leaves in pathetic handfuls.
I'm in argument with the gardener who insisted
on pruning last winter although I said it was too small.

My anger's a bud that wants to burst open
but I don't let it flower, don't say: it's your fault
the bush hasn't the strength to survive the drought.
Inwardly I fume and lament, ask myself why I feel

such longing to touch purple tassels. Is it
because those masses of tiny florets slipping
orange kisses suggest being seventeen and aching
for caresses or because the scent's a reminder to reap

redcurrants? Buddleia leans over wasteground walls,
by carparks' spiked fences, towers into trees,
thrives on unwatered, unloved gravel by decaying
railway stations in the suburbs, is unfazed by seas

of traffic. But in my garden it's shrivelled. Bees,
which have lived on this planet for millions of years,
bees, whose dwelling places humans are destroying,
have chosen to nest in our cellar. They're bearing

nectar gathered from oregano and lavender blooms
through a crack in the concrete terrace but none
have visited the dying buddleia. I'll choose a spot
for another bush when the cool season drifts in,

guard it from the gardener's secateurs, feed it water
whenever the sun beats loud on its drum. I'll dream
its honeyness and the queen wintering in her cell.
Surely next summer purple plumes will hum?

EATING WATERMELON

Heat hugs our rooms as if a huge stove's
gas jets are burning fiercely at the heart
of the house. When I open the wardrobe door

the hanging clothes give off warmth as though
they're inhabited by hot bodies. Every window,
pushed far out, could be a lolling tongue

longing for air laden with moisture that's cool.
Five o'clock. The unblinking sun won't shift
its gaze until night moths begin to flutter.

Now is the time to take the quarter of watermelon
out of the fridge. There's no word for its colour
which is too deep for pink, too gentle for red

and almost transparent. I love the faint white
rivering of veins and the certainty in the bedded rows
of black seeds. Even looking at this segment

rests light-exhausted eyes. Now is the time
to cut slices. I press one to my forehead to soothe
its throbbing, sit down at the kitchen table

in the shade of the back door's blind, lift the flesh
to my mouth. Nothing sweeter, nothing so utterly
unmalicious has ever passed down my throat.

As if I'd been immersed in a bath, I'm cooled
and revived. I wonder how a fruit can hoard
so much liquid, bring such beneficence, remember

my own body is mainly composed of water,
water that kindles life. To celebrate I consume
another slice of melon. Juice drips from my chin.

STREAM

I can't bear it – Pymmes Brook has shrunk.
It's a mulish animal and caught in its mangy coat
are long-necked bottles, leaves, rainbows of oil.

Cracks are opening in grassless patches beside it.
Every day the sun squeezes a little more sap
from the willow trees. Remembering how need

drove religion in *Henderson The Rain King* –
the long-drawn ceremonies, the obsessiveness,
I consider chanting, raising my arms, dancing

but don't. Instead I listen to the thin hish
coming from the mini-waterfall above the bridge.
How many days before it dwindles to a trickle?

Suppose the Brook shrivels up and lies
in its bed like a dead slug? Suppose the water
we assume at the flick of a tap is suddenly

cut off? Sitting by the pitiful stream, I close
my eyes, conjure fountains silking the air,
create a translucent lake lapping quietly,

plant myself by a mountain torrent. It drowns
the hammering of thought, blesses skin
with spray, roars emerald slopes, utters the birth

of a rivermouth a hundred miles away. The Brook
remains sullen but floating on it are three
furry black globes, each with a crimson tag –

moorhen chicks urged on by an anxious mother –
and two damselflies, glittering like brooches,
settle for seconds on stalks sprouting on the bank.

I'm reminded of all the life this water nourishes.
Up in the untrammelled ocean of sky is a trail
from a solitary silver fish. It's rising . . . rising.

IMAGES

The dictionary defines *viaduct*
as a structure which carries a railway
or road over a valley. But to me
viaduct is the reddish arches beside
Pymmes Brook, the cathedral aisle which slopes
upwards past the hedge of the bowling green
and the tennis courts, the slants of sunlight on walls,
on earth floors. The viaduct is guardian
of Snake Island where my child paddled
deep into imagination, it's keeper
of the park where I walk to renew myself,
where yesterday I passed the flamboyant red
of an autumn sycamore, saw whirling dots
of starlings settle in an oak that at once
became a singing tree, each bird
a note on the stave of twigs.
                                    I will never strip
the viaduct to its bare facts: the height
of its arches, dirty pink patches on bricks,
or even the stains from water trickles though
they resemble tears. It would lose meaning
like a face with perfect features does
if it's blank, without context.
                                    Think of the image
of Vivien Leigh as Aurora in long folds
of a gown rising through the fluff of mist,
a swan's wing of cloud behind her head,
her sweet downward eyes, the white garland
on her dark hair, one arm upraised, the other
stretched out as if to offer us the day.
The man who created this vision believed

suggestion was everything. He would never
have reduced a filmstar to the flesh and bones
of a woman who is ill and depressed.
                                    I share
with him the passion for a greater reality:
the vision of that goddess promising dawn,
the purplish blur of the viaduct's bricks
at dusk, the invisible rumble it carries
when little squares of light threading the darkness
bring me news that day is about to break.

The photographer of Vivien Leigh was Angus McBean

NAMING IT

As if they are paper cutouts which a giant hand
has crushed on a whim, all the buildings around me
buckle and collapse. When the dust settles

a hard white sun is crawling over
a wasteland of broken stone, a single column
is holding up half a triumphal arch. I peer

into a tower whose darkness is packed
with air that smells of decay, pass pink-
headed ranks leading lesser weeds

over tumbled masonry. Here's a slice
of house with layers which could be bedclothes
or fishing nets dangling from the upper floor.

Skirting a seashell bath mapped with cracks,
I search the ground for evidence. Not a hint
of human remains. The panic is all in the rubble.

I pick my way past a yanked tree,
try not to touch grievous roots
grappling with the air. Then I come upon it:

a pool of taintless blue which is so small
I could hold out my hands and cup it.
It's crucial to capture the exact word for its colour:

not azure, aquamarine, cobalt, turquoise.
Soon I'm uttering wildflowers in a litany:
speedwell, bugloss, vetch, forget-me-not.

I stop at harebell trembling on its wiry thread,
harebell that bends but keeps its head.
Babbling its name, I surface in another reality.

SEEING THE KINGFISHER

It may be that I stumbled
on the burning blue moment
because I'd stopped trying to find it.

One leafless December morning
as the sun sifted the uncertain air
I glimpsed blue in flight and gleaming

above the brook's polluted waters,
a sapphire blue but unlike stone
it seemed weightless, movement flinging

spectrums of colour. I thought I'd misread
magpie feathers or maybe dreamed
the bird that I'd turned into myth

but it alighted on a twig by the stream
and I saw its breast's orange swell, its blue
paler in the shade, its size smaller

than I'd expected. For one minute – two –
it perched motionless, then dived.
Heart racing, I questioned why

I'd longed to see the actual bird
when a photograph could show it larger,
more clearly. But I knew the truth:

I needed to catch sight of it alive
in the untrappable now. I walked on
through pools of sun. At the last bridge

I saw two pairs of luminous wings flying
upstream above the unruly rush
of waters muddied and swollen by rain

towards the trees by the viaduct.
Could this vision help me entertain
with calm the thought of a coming time

when my conscious body will fold away
and I'll be feather-thin images that fly
into minds and perhaps settle there?

FOX

Awakening to snow, flakes falling on
and on, their white silence swallowing
everything, even the voices always arguing

in my head; wanting the white slowly
enfolding lawns, lacing the darks of trees
to remain untouched and yet longing to touch it;

discovering a trail of prints that passes
our back door, sunk sets of four toes –
a sign, not of dog, but fox looking for food.

It ignored the black bucket, didn't ravage
rotten cabbages, apple skins – the forage
was for flesh threaded with blood.

Suddenly it leaps from a pocket of memory –
that fox secreted over five decades ago,
the one that emerged from a clump on the Downs,

smaller than fox was in my imagination,
its coat not vermilion or red, not sienna,
not orange or tawny though fox is all of these,

but muted somehow, dusty in the heat.
In its mouth a bloodied pheasant, head bitten,
feathers mashed. Unblinking, it eyed me

for a minute then loped off into the trees . . .
Foxes rooting in the suburbs are too easy
to seize on but this one that rubbed past my wall

and sniffed the warmth indoors, was no cliché.
I believe it wanted in with its pointed ears, its eyes
gleaming amber but offering nothing.

And I want to open door and window, pull it in –
that bracken-red fur, the stealth, even
the inescapable smell. I need fox, its hungers

to inhabit my body, tighten my throat.
And when I've made it my own the wrangling
will stop and I'll set foot on the wide white.

BREGMACEROS ALBYI

A mere strip, it could easily be missed
or mistaken for a willow leaf but if I run
a finger down the line in the middle

I can feel the spine's indentation.
And look, it's hatched with bones fine
as hairs, its fins fan like minute wings.

The whiskers could be fuzzing a ripe
barley stalk but through a glass I see
that they rise from the rounded head

and I peer at the eye still staring
from the dark of its socket. The mouth
at last gasp is a cave gaping with ever.

Why did I want to buy this piece
of past so precisely stamped on stone?
Did I believe owning it would offer me

an open sesame to time, that I'd unravel
the bracelets of months, travel beyond
decades, centuries, millennia, arrive

at the point five million years ago
when this creature lived? Did I believe
putting this fossil in my favourite room

would relate it to my self with its swamp
of feelings, black hole of fear, its griefs
and firefly moments? Did I fool myself

into thinking that this once flesh, blood
and breath would make me feel a sense
of continuity? Whichever shelf I put it on

it remains utterly distant and yet its imprint
has survived. No one can tell what
will be obliterated, what leave its mark.

THE OYSTER SHELL

for John

is ajar but still tightly hinged.
From inside, where pale colours
drift to deep, a sense of secret
rises – I don't want to break it.

Instead I finger the outer hump,
its solid waves ribbed and marbled
with mauve – not waves, troubled rocks
or stiffened sleeves with many folds,

overlapping tongues, rucks in the head
of a dead monster that stinks of fish.
Why am I fabricating? In this cave
a tiny mussel is attached by thread

to the curved wall. On its uneven floor
is a minute frond and a sand pellet
which contains no pearl. Once,
a soft-bodied creature stirred

within the mantle's protective skin,
changed sex – a life-system quite unlike
the human, as persistent. In my mind
I again dig the shell out of sand

wet from a sea that's releasing miles
of beach. Then I stare at the sky's blue.
Beyond it light from unnumbered suns
traverses an immeasurable dark and I know,

as I've never known before, a power
beyond the human brain's grasp exists
in the universe, a power that knits
random with pattern. And I know prayer

won't reveal its language. Reeling
at the rim of terrible excitement,
I retreat to the cradle of this shell,
creep in, unclothe my self, tread

on milkwhite and mother-of pearl,
follow faint pools of sandgold
to the sullen indigo sea lying below
the hinge at its core. Here, I let go.

THIS ROSE

after 'The Rose' by Mae Holsgrove

is a revelation. Peer
   through the compressions
      and the releases in its many layers

to segments that are pink
   and purple – you will make out
         a snake coiling in on itself to make a maze.

Follow the concentric paths
   led by pointed leaves – you'll wonder
      why they travel with such determination.

You can see the beginnings
   of shapes that are still inexplicable.
      This black speck might be a tadpole

in a bubble of spawn
   or the eye of a fledgling in an egg.
      Something is waiting to be pulled out,

threaded with breath, wrapped
   in light. Will you try and discover
      the intention or if there is an intention?

Lines you have read,
   your own lines of thought,
      your intuitions may illumine a route

through these circles
   with the intense blue which burns
      in the flame of a match that's struck

in a dark room.
    But the further in you go,
        the nearer you come to the mystery

at the crimson heart
    where *word* is not divided
        from *rose*, the deeper you see it is.